T0294300

BOND VEHICLE COLLECTIBLES

Paul Brent Adams

AMBERLEY

To Keith Marshall, whose help and kindness really made a difference – thank you.

Photographic Credit
I would like to thank Vectis Auctions in the UK for supplying many excellent photographs from their archives for this book, which has allowed some of the rarer items to be illustrated.

First published 2017

Amberley Publishing
The Hill, Stroud
Gloucestershire, GL5 4EP

www.amberley-books.com

Copyright © Paul Brent Adams, 2017

The right of Paul Brent Adams to be identified as the Author of this work has been asserted in accordance with the Copyrights, Designs and Patents Act 1988.

ISBN 978 1 4456 7038 6 (print)
ISBN 978 1 4456 7039 3 (ebook)

British Library Cataloguing in Publication Data.
A catalogue record for this book is available from the British Library.

Origination by Amberley Publishing.
Printed in the UK.

Contents

Introduction

James Bond is the most famous secret agent in the world, so it is only fitting that he should drive some of the most famous cars in the world – such as the Aston Martin DB5 'with modifications'. In fact Mr Bond and his adversaries have had a whole fleet of gadget-packed spy cars and other vehicles to choose from over the years; everything from a milk float to the Space Shuttle. Many of these Motor Stars are available in model form, allowing us all to own our favourite Bond vehicles: the DB5 from *Goldfinger*; the Lotus submarine car from *The Spy Who Loved Me*; or the Russian Army T-55 tank from *GoldenEye*.

While there is plenty of Bond film memorabilia to collect, here we are going to concentrate largely on diecast models. If you think this is a very small slice of the Bond empire, think again. Literally hundreds of diecast models have already been produced, and each new film sees another batch. To collect everything would require considerable dedication, plenty of shelf space and deep pockets, but a wide and varied collection can still be built up, even without the highly priced rarities.

One thing that may surprise many is how little driving Bond actually does in many of the films. Frequently he is a passenger, or a prisoner. It has even been claimed that there are two films in which he does not drive at all, but this is incorrect. In *You Only Live*

Where it all began – the first Corgi James Bond Aston Martin DB5, model 261 from *Goldfinger*, released in October 1965. Even the card tray holding the model was packed with excitement, and an envelope containing Secret Instructions. (Vectis Auctions)

Twice, Bond is driving the Toyota 2000GT as its approaches Henderson's house, even though Aki had been behind the wheel seconds before – perhaps a simple continuity error. In *Moonraker*, having escaped from beneath Moonraker 5, Bond and Holly rush to get aboard Moonraker 6, using a small yellow runabout – which is left-hand drive, so Bond is driving. He has also used many boats, and every conceivable type of aircraft.

Nearly half a century after *Goldfinger*, Hot Wheels in America released their version of the DB5, and Italeri from Italy produced the AW101 helicopter seen in *Skyfall*.

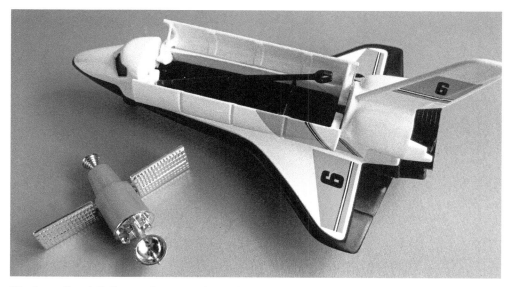

The James Bond Collection from 1997 featured reissues of several older Corgi models, including the Moonraker Space Shuttle from 1979. This had a retractable undercarriage, opening cargo bay doors, and a satellite as the payload. There was also a smaller version in the Juniors series.

Collecting Bond

The Birth of Bond

The first Bond novel, *Casino Royale*, appeared in 1953, and was adapted for American television the following year. Ian Fleming (1908–64) would eventually write twelve Bond novels, and two short story collections, with the adventures of his character being continued by other writers after his death. The first Bond film appeared in 1962, and the total is now up to twenty-six. Of these, twenty-four have been made by Eon Productions. There was also a cartoon series.

Diecasts and Star Cars

Diecast model vehicles are cast in heavy metal moulds called dies, hence the term. They appeared just before the First World War, becoming well established in the post-war years. Toy production in Britain was halted by the Second World War, but resumed once peace returned, with many new diecasting firms appearing. Corgi arrived in 1956 and were the first to offer clear plastic windows – an exciting new gimmick in the 1950s. Until then, diecasts had been nearly all cast metal, perhaps with rubber wheels or tyres. By the 1960s nearly all diecasts included plastic parts: windows, interiors and various accessories. A major advantage of plastic over metal was that it could be moulded in any colour required, and did not need painting. By the mid-1960s the major diecast companies were offering ever more detailed and accurate models, with an increasing number of working features. Then came models based on popular films and television shows known as Star Cars or Character Cars. Such models had actually been around since the 1930s, but did not make an impact until much later. Corgi released their first Bond model in 1965, and except for a brief break in the 1980s, they have been producing them ever since. These early Star Cars were all produced as toys for children, but since the 1990s many have been aimed at adult collectors. The decade or so after the reappearance of Bond in 1995, after an absence of six years, saw an explosion of new models, many coming from companies venturing into the world of Bond for the first time.

Scale

Scale is the size of a model relative to the object it is based on. This can be given as a ratio – 1:36, or a fraction – 1/43. The larger the number, the smaller the model. Most models are made to a limited number of standard scales. As cars are fairly small, they tend to be made to fairly large scales: 1:18, 1:36, 1:43; or 1:64 for the smaller lines. Among model car collectors 1:43 is probably the most popular of the larger scales; the models in the James Bond Car Collection are mainly 1:43. Corgi models were initially 1:43, or a little smaller. In the 1970s they moved up to 1:36. The smallest of the main collecting scales for model cars is 1:64, which is more popular in America than in Britain. Some ranges, such as Matchbox and Corgi Juniors, are only approximately to this size, while other lines really are 1:64.

Being smaller than cars, motorcycles are generally made to much larger scales. Trucks and buses, bigger in real life, are generally made to smaller scales. Mixing scales can result in a small sports car being the same size as a double-decker bus. There are also a few models made to 'odd' scales that do not fit neatly into this system. Aircraft are usually large, and the scales tend to be smaller still. Boats and ships also vary greatly in size, and scale. Normally, collectors like to keep to just one or two scales, but

The largest and smallest of the Corgi Aston Martin DB5 models, in 1:36 and 1:64 – the larger the number the smaller the model. Both have working ejector seats.

The Corgi Ultimate Bond Collection from 2002 contained twenty-one models, a mixture of new releases and reissues. The cars were either 1:43 or 1:36, while the larger vehicles were clearly made to much smaller scales. (Vectis Auctions)

this is not really possible with Bond models – as you will soon see. Now let's see what size a DB5 is in the main model car scales:

1:8	571 mm	22 ½ inches
1:18	254 mm	10 inches
1:24	190 mm	7½ inches
1:32	143 mm	5⅝ inches
1:36	127 mm	5 inches
1:43	106 mm	4⅛ inches
1:50	91 mm	3⅝ inches
1:64	71 mm	2¾ inches
1:76	60 mm	2⅓ inches
1:87	52 mm	2 inches

Figures

Early Corgi Star Cars all included well-painted plastic figures. Later figures were less well finished, and by the late 1970s figures were no longer being included with Bond models, except for the DB5, which still needed a villain to fire into orbit. *The James Bond Collection* from 1997 each included a metal 54 mm (1:32) figure of Bond, a Bond

The James Bond Collection models from 1997 all came with a metal 54 mm figure. In the case of the Toyota 2000GT it was villain Ernst Stavro Blofeld. The original plastic figures in the car were also included.

Many of the models in *The James Bond Car Collection* partwork came with well-detailed figures. Here Mary Goodnight gives Bond, and his suitcase, a lift in her MGB, a scene from *The Man With The Golden Gun.*

Girl, or a villain. This is a popular size among figure collectors, but all were out of scale with the vehicles they accompanied. Further 54 mm figures were available separately. Modern toys and collector models seldom include figures. An exception was the JBCC: many of the models came with figures, which really helped bring the vehicles to life.

Boxes

Boxes not only protect a model, and keep any small parts and accessories together, vintage box art adds considerably to the appeal of old toys. They also provide a great deal of useful information about the models. Early boxes were all cardboard, with artwork depicting the model inside. By the 1970s the window box, with a clear plastic panel in the side, was almost universal. Today, small models usually come in a clear plastic bubble, on a backing card. Models aimed at collectors and partwork models often come in clear plastic display cases with lift-off lids. The models are usually firmly screwed to the base. Corgi have produced a number of multi-vehicle sets in circular tins, resembling a film canister, which come in an outer cardboard box. The boxes used for modern adult collectable models are often very dull compared to boxes from the 1960s. Thankfully, some collector models have gone back to using colourful, vintage-style box art.

Corgi boxes from the 1960s were all card, and were adorned with colourful graphics. They showed the film car in action, and listed the features of the model within. This is the Toyota 2000GT from 1967, the second Corgi Bond model. (Vectis Auctions)

By the 1970s and 1980s window boxes were in vogue and artwork was less important as the model inside was now visible. Boxes from the Roger Moore era made extensive use of his portrait, like this Corgi Citroen 2CV. (Vectis Auctions)

Small models are now generally sold in clear plastic bubbles, glued to a backing card. Hot Wheels models, such as the Lotus Esprit S1 road car, can be found on both long and short cards.

Modern boxes aimed at adult collectors are often very dull compared with those from the 1960s, such as this Corgi DB10 from *Spectre*.

Screen Accuracy

How closely does a model match the vehicles on screen? Sometimes small or delicate parts are omitted, or made over-scale for strength. Complex colour schemes and markings may be simplified to make them easier to apply. Especially with toy lines, an existing model may be painted to match a screen vehicle, even if it is not exactly the right type, or year – in some cases it is not even close. The telephone van used by the character Jaws in *The Spy Who Loved Me* was a Leyland Sherpa, but the Corgi Junior model was based on an American Chevrolet van, while Johnny Lightning used a Ford van for their model – and neither had a roof rack. Only the JBCC model is a Sherpa. Some errors are not the fault of the model companies; if the filmmakers have used different vehicles when shooting a film, these can sometimes differ. The Ford station wagon in *From Russia With Love* is a four-door version when it first appears at the Gypsy camp, but a two-door model in a later scene. In *Licence to Kill* the Dodge Ram pickup initially has aluminium-coloured door mirrors, which later mysteriously change to black. Often extra James Bond or 007 logos will be added to models, which were not carried on screen. Even villain cars may carry 007 number plates. In the early days of diecasts such markings were usually applied using paper stickers or decals. Today, tampo printing is the most common method, wherein ink is applied to pads, which then apply it to the model.

Models sold as toys often have extra markings, such as the 007 logos on these Corgi and Corgi Junior versions of the Lotus Esprit submarine car. The 1970s Junior has a paper label, while the larger version is a reissue with the 007 logo printed directly onto the model.

The Bond Library

There is no shortage of reference books or internet sites on Bond, some being devoted entirely to Bond cars. The major types are well covered, but information on minor vehicles can be harder to find – and not all of it is accurate. *The James Bond Car Collection*, a partwork devoted to Bond models, included many such vehicles, and is a very useful reference. Many books do not cover the two non-Eon films – the 1967 version of *Casino Royale*, and *Never Say Never Again*. Then there are the films themselves, which we can now watch over and over again, and in slow motion, thanks to video and DVD. There has only been one previous book on Bond models. *The James Bond Diecasts of Corgi*, by Dave Worrall, appeared in 1996, just before the 1990s explosion in Bond models. A tiny booklet, again by Dave Worrall, was included with the Corgi DB5 set, bringing the story up to 2007.

Building a Collection

Current models can be bought in toy and model shops. Lines aimed at collectors are generally only available in specialist model shops. Obsolete models are those no longer in production, and are not available in shops, although other versions of the same basic casting may still be available. With a popular subject such as Bond, many models are reissued – if the company still has the licence – often with slight differences between versions. Some model shops carry second-hand models, and there is the internet, but you cannot examine the models on offer. The best place to find obsolete models, and see them up close, is at a collectors' fair. These are usually regular events. Ensure the fair is still on before setting out, and if you rely on public transport, check this too. Arrive early; equip yourself with a large, sturdy bag, but not a backpack; plenty of small notes and coins; and set yourself a budget. Prices often vary from stall to stall, and some sellers will give a discount if you buy several items. Generally, the rarest and most expensive items are sold by auction – there are several companies that hold specialist toy sales several times a year.

In collecting, condition is one of the most important factors affecting price, with Mint in Box or Mint on Card being the ideal. However, if you are prepared to accept unboxed models, or those showing some signs of wear, prices come down considerably. In a way, it is nice to know that someone has actually played with, and enjoyed, a model, rather than leaving it sitting in a cupboard for fifty years.

When it comes to taking care of your collection, models should be kept out of direct sunlight, which can fade both the model and its packaging, and affect plastic parts. Avoid dampness. Dust can be a problem if models are displayed on open shelves. Never use a normal duster on models, instead use a large, soft artist's paintbrush, a soft make-up brush, or a puffer brush used for cleaning cameras and computers. Make sure your shelving can take the weight of the models, as diecasts are heavy. This includes checking the supports the shelves rest on, as some plastic supports can shear off. Because most model vehicles have wheels, they can roll off a shelf, and fall to the floor. Either add a lip to the shelf, or lift the model up, so its wheels do not actually touch the shelf.

The Manufacturers

Several firms have produced Bond models over the years, but usually only for short periods, with the exception of Corgi, who have been making Bond models for over half a century. In the early days new models were always tied to the latest film, except for the gadget-packed DB5, which has been an essential part of almost any Bond range. Since the late 1990s manufacturers have gone back over the Bond series and released models of vehicles not previously covered: in some cases from films that had been missed at the time. Existing models were also reissued. Despite this, there are still a number of gaps, especially for the two non-Eon films. These gaps can be filled by using non-Bond models, if they are of the correct vehicle type, although the colours and markings may not exactly match the screen vehicles.

Corgi

Corgi were not the first to produce toys based on films or television shows but no one else put as much effort into them as Corgi did. Their first Star Car was an existing model painted to represent the car driven by a television crime-fighter known as the Saint, played by Roger Moore. The Saint's Volvo P1800 came out in March 1965. Corgi had not produced a Bond model when *Goldfinger* was released in 1964, but after seeing how successful the film was they decided to get a model out in time for Christmas 1965, just before the next Bond film appeared. This model, the James Bond Aston Martin DB5, was only their second Star Car, but it would sell millions over the next few years, and help to establish toy Star Cars. Corgi are still producing versions of the DB5 today, in several sizes.

Corgi would go on to produce models for most of the Bond films up until the early 1980s. Apart from the eternally popular DB5, most of these were only available for a limited time – perhaps just a year or two – before being retired. Financial problems would see the company lose the Bond licence for a time to Matchbox, but regain it in the 1990s. Finally they began to reissue some of their older, retired models. The James Bond Collection appeared in 1997, and included seven models. Apart from the DB5, most of these had been unavailable since the 1970s or 1980s. All came in special silver and black boxes, and included a metal figure. This series was so successful that Corgi launched more reissues, and began producing new models based on the older Bond films, not just the current release. While most of these have been to 1:36 scale, there has been the odd model to 1:43, and larger vehicles such as trucks and buses have been made to smaller scales still. In 2003 the Showcase collection appeared, comprising an initial eight models that were much smaller than regular Corgis, but still larger than the old Juniors. Corgi continue to reissue their older models, although not everything is available at once.

There have been a number of Limited Edition models, of which only a specified number are produced – this is usually given on the packaging, and some include a Limited Edition certificate. An anniversary is another good excuse to reissue an existing model in a new box, and some of these too have been Limited Editions. The year 2007 was obviously a good time to issue some more special models, and there appeared several two-vehicle sets for the Sean Connery, Roger Moore and Pierce Brosnan eras, as well as a DB5 set with both old and new versions of the car. There have also been a number of gold-plated models, in gold-coloured chrome. While intended as special models, they are hardly screen accurate. There have also been a very small number of real gold-plated models, produced for presentation to VIPs at film premieres. When such rare models turn up at auction, they command very high prices. Very few collectors could ever hope to own such a model.

Husky, Corgi Junior, and Rockets

To compete with Matchbox, Corgi launched the small-scale Husky range in 1964, sold exclusively in Woolworths. Star Cars were added in 1967 as Husky Extras. Once the deal with Woolworths ended, the Huskys were renamed Corgi Juniors in 1970. Eventually the Junior part of the name was dropped, but collectors still refer to these smaller models as Juniors to avoid confusing them with their larger counterparts, as a number of models existed in both sizes, including several Bond cars. Corgi Rockets were a short-lived range introduced in late 1969. They had a detachable chassis, and ran on plastic track like Hot Wheels. In fact Mattel sued Corgi, and the entire Rockets range soon disappeared. Several Bond models appeared in either the Junior or Rockets ranges. Much later, Corgi would again produce a range of small-scale Bond models, but these were the same as those made by the American firm Johnny Lightning, although with different bases. There were ten cars in this series, matching the first batch of JL models, although there were actually only eight castings, as the DB5 and Lotus Esprit each appeared in two versions.

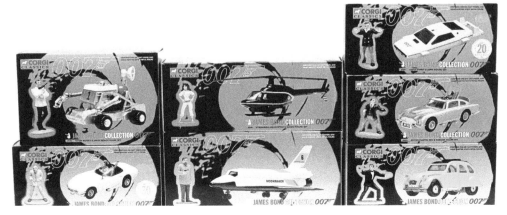

The first Corgi reissues of older Bond models appeared in 1997, in these black and silver boxes. The Lotus and Toyota were also promoted as 20th and 30th Anniversary models. (Vectis Auctions)

A modern version of the 1:43 Corgi DB5, in a 1960s-style box. The same model was available in a standard version, and as a *Goldfinger* 50th Anniversary model, followed by a *Thunderball* 50th Anniversary edition. Both gold and silver versions were produced, with the silver being more common. (Vectis Auctions)

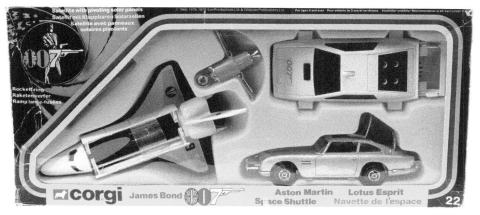

Corgi were very fond of producing sets, including this one containing models from three Bond films – all are standard models that were also available individually. (Vectis Auctions)

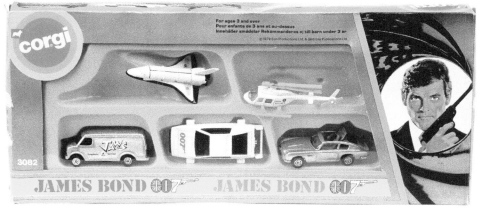

This Corgi Juniors set also contains models from three films, but adds the Drax Airlines Jetranger helicopter from *Moonraker*, which was another standard model; and the Jaws telephone repair van, which was only included in this set, and another devoted entirely to *The Spy Who Loved Me*. (Vectis Auctions)

Corgi have always been especially fond of releasing models in multi-vehicle sets, Bond included. Some were included in general film and television crime-fighter sets, others were devoted entirely to Bond. Some mixed models from several different films, others were devoted to a single film. Occasionally models that were not available individually were included in these sets. In the 1970s and 1980s several vehicles were available in both regular and Junior versions. Taking advantage of this, Corgi released a number of Little and Large sets in the early 1980s, including several Bond sets.

Matchbox

Matchbox models first appeared in 1953, but the company never took much interest in Star Cars. When Corgi ran into difficulties in the 1980s, Matchbox briefly picked up the Bond licence, beginning with *A View To A Kill*, but really did very little with it. There were no models for *The Living Daylights*, and only a rather poor set for *Licence To Kill*. Other models were planned, but did not go beyond a few prototypes, which occasionally appear at auction. Some collectors have filled in the gaps themselves by modifying existing models, or making their own Bond boxes for regular models.

Johnny Lightning

Made by Topper Toys in the USA, Johnny Lightning was a short-lived competitor to Hot Wheels; they only lasted from 1969 to 1971. In 1994 the name was revived by Playing Mantis, initially with copies of the original Topper models. A range of 1:64 scale Bond cars was launched in the late 1990s. Early releases, in three batches, were all cars. Later the range was expanded for the 40th Anniversary of the Bond films, with a wider selection of models. There were also two-model and four-model sets. Apart from the regular issues, there were special White Lightning versions of the later models (but

The Johnny Lightning *Goldfinger* set depicts the scene where Tilly Masterson is killed by Oddjob, and Bond is captured. It contains two vehicles and three figures. (Vectis Auctions)

In addition to single models, JL produced three four-vehicle sets. Heroic Horsepower (Bond cars), Ravishing Ragtops (convertibles), and Villainous Vehicles (villain cars). (Vectis Auctions)

not the first batch). These had the name White Lightning on the wheels, and some part of the model in white – they were aimed at collectors who had to have every variant of a model, no matter how minor, and were only produced in small numbers, mixed in with the regular models. JL eventually covered all the Eon films up to *Die Another Day*, but there were only one or two models per film. Corgi later reissued the first batch of JL models, in new packaging, but did not follow up with the later models.

Hot Wheels

Owned by Mattel (who now also own Matchbox), Hot Wheels were launched in 1968. They had thin axles, and lightweight wheels, making them very fast. The company took little interest in Star Cars until the early 2000s. Their first Bond models appeared in 2014. A few models have appeared in the standard toy range, known as the Mainline, with the title of the film in one corner of the backing card. In 2015 there was a five-model Bond set, on special cards. Most models have appeared in the HW Entertainment line, aimed at adult collectors. Introduced in 2013 as Retro Entertainment, this series focused exclusively on film and television models. These are either enhanced versions of models from the toy line, with metal rather than plastic bases, more realistic Real Rider wheels, and more detailed tampo printing, or special models or variants. They cost four to five times as much as Mainline toys. There have also been some very large, highly detailed, and expensive 1:18 scale models, and a few mid-sized models in 1:43.

Hot Wheels produce several ranges of models aimed at collectors. The Entertainment series of film and television models includes several Bond cars, such as the Ford Mustang Mach 1 used in *Diamonds Are Forever*.

The James Bond Car Collection

This was a fortnightly partwork, comprising a model and a magazine giving background information on the Bond films and vehicles. It was issued by Eaglemoss in Britain, beginning in 2007, and was also available in several other countries. The series was extended several times, and eventually ran for 134 regular issues; there were also three special 'Gift' models only available to subscribers. The models were actually made by Universal Hobbies, joined later by Ixo. The bulk were made to the popular collecting scale of 1:43, with a few exceptions. Most were cars, but there were some very unusual models included in the range, and many of the vehicles are not available as official Bond models from anyone else. All but two of the Gift models came in clear plastic display cases (which can be a little fragile), and were set in a small diorama depicting a particular scene from the film they appeared in, with a printed background. Some were shown with 'damage' or gadgets deployed. These dioramas really enhance the models, and some are very detailed. Several vehicles appeared more than once, in different versions. All the Eon films up to *Skyfall* were included, but sadly not the two non-Eon films. The number of models per film also varied, from one up to eleven.

The James Bond Car Collection was a partwork devoted entirely to Bond models. All came in clear plastic display cases. This DB5 is from *Thunderball*, and is fitted with twin water jets.

This was certainly the best partwork ever released, and the models were to a very high standard, despite the odd error. Initially costing just £7.99 each, they are still widely available at fairs and online, although you may have to pay a little more now. The series has been reissued, at least in certain areas, as Bond in Motion. Many of the models shown here are from this series, with the clear plastic top removed to show the models and their settings more clearly.

James Bond's DB5 is another partwork by Eaglemoss. This time a giant 1:8 scale DB5 is supplied in kit form, in metal and plastic, with all the equipment fitted to the *Goldfinger* car, even the items that are not seen on screen. The finished model is 571 mm long, and weighs 8.5 kg. There were eighty-six issues, and the model was so complex there was an instructional DVD with Issue 1 showing how to put it all together. I still have not tackled mine – my excuse is I need a bigger table.

Minor Players

Many of the companies that have produced Bond models have done so for only a short period. Others have not made any official Bond items, but have released non-Bond models that can be used to fill in some of the gaps in a Bond collection.

ERTL is an American company best known for their farm toys. They later branched out into other areas, such as aircraft and Star Cars, including a small range dedicated to the cartoon series *James Bond Jr.*

Micro Machines, made by the American company Galoob, were a range of really tiny vehicles and figures. They were sold in sets, rather than individually, due to their small size. Three Bond sets were released in the 1990s, covering *Goldfinger*, *The Spy*

Shell petrol stations in Britain ran a Bond model promotion involving vehicles from *Dr No* to *Quantum of Solace*. The briefcase with a clear side is thought to be a sample case. (Vectis Auctions)

Among the companies producing higher priced Bond models aimed at collectors is Minichamps, whose range includes both single models and sets in various scales. (Vectis Auctions)

Who Loved Me and *Moonraker*. Each contained three vehicles and two figures, and there was a combined set with everything. Some of the vehicles were not modelled by anyone else, such as one of the planes from Pussy Galore's Flying Circus in *Goldfinger*. Shell petrol stations in Britain ran a Bond promotion that included several small-scale cars. Each came in a small plastic display case, and included a miniature copy of the film poster.

BMW are best known for building real cars, but while providing vehicles for the films during the Pierce Brosnan era, they released a number of Bond models in BMW boxes. The models were actually manufactured by other companies. Boats and ships have featured heavily in many Bond films, but few have been modelled. Tri-ang Minic Ships were a range of small, 1:1200 scale, diecast waterline model ships and harbour accessories produced from 1959 to 1964. Part of the range was revived by Hornby in the 1970s and a modern series is now available. Purely by coincidence, several of the models have a Bond connection, and are worth looking out for. Finally, there are a number of firms making higher priced models aimed only at collectors, generally in the larger scales, from 1:43 up to 1:18. However, such ranges are generally confined to the most popular 'glamour cars', and the selection is limited.

Kits

Plastic car kits are generally larger than their diecast counterparts, but there have not been many Bond vehicles. In the 1960s Airfix in Britain did a few in 1:24 scale, while the American company Aurora made an unofficial Aston Martin Super Spy Car in the American scale of 1:25. Much later Airfix and Revell both produced kits for *Moonraker*. More recently the Italian firm Italeri have produced a Bond kit. There have also been a number of Japanese kits, which can be hard to find outside Japan, and are expensive. The main role of plastic kits is going to be in-filling the many gaps that exist in the range of aircraft and ship models available – Airfix have produced many useful models over the years. A little experience in modelling is going to help here. One problem with kits is that in this case 'Mint in Box' means unbuilt, so an assembled model is never going to be mint.

An unbuilt Airfix DB5 kit in 1:24, with a classic example of 1960s Airfix box art. This model could be built stock if desired. (Vectis Auctions)

From America, the unofficial Aurora Super Spy Car in 1:25, which managed to avoid mentioning James Bond anywhere on the packaging or the instruction sheet. (Vectis Auctions)

Slot Cars

Gilbert was a major American toymaker, and for Christmas 1965 they produced what must be one of the most magnificent toys ever made. It was a James Bond 007 Road Race set, depicting winding mountain roads, with '16 thrill-packed obstacles', including a washed out bridge. The landscape comprised six moulded plastic sections that clipped together, and measured an impressive 34 x 51 inches, or 86 x 129 centimetres. The set included a blue DB5 and a red Ford Mustang fastback (rather than the white convertible from *Goldfinger*). Problems with the set meant that many were returned and the cost of these returns has been blamed for putting Gilbert out of business.

Over the years there have been a number of more conventional slot car sets and individual models related to James Bond, from companies such as Scalextric in Britain and Carrera in Germany. The first Scalextric set appeared in 1967, and contained a white DB5 complete with ejector seat, and a black Mercedes 190SL. Given the hard life these working models lead, their chances of survival are low, making them rare and expensive today.

Martin, Aston Martin –
The Classic DB5

In the novel *Goldfinger* (1959), Bond drives an Aston Martin DB Mark III, but in the film he uses the latest DB5. Two cars were used for filming. The main 'gadget car' was a prototype DB5, modified from a DB4. For *Goldfinger* it was fitted with an array of special equipment, not all of which was used on screen. In the scene where Q is explaining the control switches to Bond, he does not explain what they all do, only those that will actually be used later in the film.

The car crashes during its mission in Switzerland, but must have been recovered and repaired, because it appears again in *Thunderball*. George Lazenby drives the later DBS in *On Her Majesty's Secret Service*. Roger Moore never drove an Aston Martin in his time as Bond. It would not be until *GoldenEye*, in 1995, that Bond would again be seen at the wheel of a DB5. The car subsequently appeared in *Tomorrow Never Dies*, and very briefly in *The World Is Not Enough*. Its main scene in the film was cut, but can be found on the Special Features disc of the two-disc DVD edition, arriving at a funeral; near the end of the film it appears on a monitor screen, as M is trying to locate Bond. The DB5 appears again in *Casino Royale*, *Skyfall* and *Spectre*. The DB5 used in *Casino Royale* is a standard, albeit left-hand drive car, which Bond wins at the gambling tables. In later films the DB5 is outfitted with the gadgets from *Goldfinger*, although they do not see much use. In *Skyfall* it is blown up during the final battle, but is again repaired in time for *Spectre*. A number of different real cars have been used over the years.

The Models

It is the universal opinion of every small boy who ever owned one, no matter how old they might be now, that the Corgi Aston Martin DB5 was one of the best toys ever made. Certainly, everyone remembers the working ejector seat. Corgi had produced a 1:46 scale DB4 in 1960, followed by a Competition (racing) version in 1962. This was the first Corgi model with a lift-up bonnet and engine detail. The car came in either yellow with a red interior, or red with a yellow interior; the racer was green and white, with various racing numbers. When Corgi decided to produce the James Bond DB5, they modified the existing DB4, although the work involved was considerable. This did lead to an error, with the first model retaining the tail lights of the DB4, but these were changed to the DB5 type on later models.

The opening bonnet and engine were dropped, but model 261 gained pop-out machine guns and front bumper over-riders, operated by the front catch on the left side of the model. A working ejector seat fired its unfortunate passenger through an opening hatch in the roof, operated by the rear catch. The bulletproof screen at the rear popped up when the exhaust pipe was pushed in. All this in a model only 97 mm long. Wire-spoke wheels were fitted, and a plastic figure of James Bond was added behind the wheel. Two plastic villains were included, in case one got lost; and if both were lost there was an accessory pack available containing two more. This model was painted gold, rather than silver. This is generally explained as Corgi not wanting a silver model to appear unpainted. Honestly, I doubt this. The film was called *Goldfinger*, and it was about a bullion heist, so painting the model gold would have made perfect sense.

In 1968 a new, slightly larger DB5 was introduced, replacing the earlier version – it actually had the word 'new' cast into the baseplate. Model 270 was 1:43 scale, making it 102 mm long, and it had even more features than the first model. Finger-operated revolving number plates front and rear and extending plastic tyre slashers on both rear wheels were fitted in addition to all the features of the original. This time the model was painted silver, matching the movie car. In the late 1960s Corgi changed over to low-friction Whizzwheels, which appeared on both new and existing models. These were less realistic than the older wheel designs, but gave better performance. Both full-size and Junior models were affected.

Corgi again increased the size of their models in the 1970s, switching to 1:36, making their existing 1:43 models look tiny, including the DB5. So a new version was produced in 1978 in 1:36, as 271. There were several changes from the previous version. The revolving number plates and tyre slashers were dropped, but all the original features were retained. The machine guns were moved from the wings to the grille. This left two large holes when the guns were retracted. The first two Aston Martins only had bumper overriders at the front, but the 1:36 version had overriders on the rear bumper as well. Pressing on the rear overriders now operated the rear bulletproof screen.

In the 1990s and later the 1:43 version of the DB5 was reissued, but several detail changes show that a different die was being used. The current small version is something of a hybrid, combining features of the 1965 and 1968 versions. Over the years some reissues have been painted gold, like the original model from 1965, with some issues being painted in both colours. Models are generally supplied to shops in an outer carton of six, and at one stage Corgi were sending out five silver models and one gold model per carton, making the gold version artificially rarer than its silver counterpart. This really annoyed a lot of people.

Yet another new DB5 appeared to tie-in with *Casino Royale*. Again in 1:36 scale, this depicted a normal road car, without all the spy gadgets, and had opening doors. Like the film car, it also had left-hand drive. This was included in a twin-pack with the earlier 1:36 DB5 spy car. To depict the DB5 as it appeared in later films, the model was changed to right-hand drive. The spy car version was a lot more fun.

The only Bond model included in the small-scale Husky range was the James Bond Aston Martin, but Corgi updated it to a DB6, a version Bond never drove. However, the only differences between the DB5 and DB6 are around the tail, so it still looked like the screen car. Despite its small size, the Husky also had a working ejector seat, but with the control catch on the right side. In 1970 the model became a Corgi Junior. Other small-scale Corgi DB5 models have been the reissued Johnny Lightning model, which came on both *Thunderball* and *GoldenEye* cards, as did the JL original, and the slightly larger Showcase version, which lacked any special features.

Apart from Corgi, almost everyone who has had a Bond range has produced a DB5, often releasing the same model in different packaging to tie-in with the many different films it has appeared in. Johnny Lightning managed four versions, and Hot Wheels have also done several. The JBCC included four: two for *Goldfinger*, and one each for *Thunderball* and *Skyfall*. Most depicted the car deploying its different gadgets.

From 1960, the original Corgi Aston Martin DB4 in 1:46, with opening bonnet, detailed engine, plain wheel hubs and no driver figure. Corgi would modify this model to produce the James Bond DB5 in 1965.

The later *James Bond Collection* version of the 1:43 DB5 from 1997, in gold. The ejector seat is the thing everyone who had one remembers.

Even the little Husky model, actually a DB6, had a working ejector seat. Later this became a Corgi Junior model, and was available in several sets.

Two versions of the 1:43 DB5; slight differences show they came from different dies. The pop-out machine guns are correctly mounted in the wings.

Again there are differences at the rear. Pushing in on the exhaust pipes activated the rear bulletproof screen.

Plastic tyre slashers on the rear wheels were added to the second Corgi DB5 in 1968, but were not included on the larger 1:36 model. They had to be pulled out by hand.

The 1:36 DB5 from 1978 moved the machine guns from the wings to the grille, which left very large openings when the guns were retracted.

There were further changes at the rear. Overriders were added to the rear bumper; pushing these in now operated the rear bulletproof screen.

The 1:36 DB5 had the same working features as the smaller 1965 model, but omitted those added to the 1968 version.

In 2007 Corgi produced a Limited Edition DB5 set containing two 1:36 scale models: the large *Goldfinger* car from 1978; and the new *Casino Royale* model with opening doors. There is also a booklet on the history of Corgi Bond models up to 2007 by Dave Worrall – but the binding is very poor – and a Limited Edition certificate stating that this is one of only 1,500 sets.

The *Casino Royale* version of the new DB5 had left-hand drive, which was correct for the film car, while later versions had right-hand drive.

One of four versions of the DB5 included in the JBCC – the ejector seat has been fired, and the machine guns are deployed. There are even bullet marks on the windscreen. The vehicle type, and film title, are given on the base.

The Films

Dr No (1962), Sean Connery

Bond has his first encounter with the villainous organisation Spectre. There are no exotic gadgets, although Bond has his Italian Beretta pistol replaced with a 7.65 mm Walter PPK. Bond is picked up from the airport by a 1957 Chevrolet Bel Air convertible; after a battle with the driver, this becomes the first car he drives on screen. He later uses a Sunbeam Alpine, which is the first real 'Bond Car', despite its lack of gadgets. There were no contemporary models for this film, and it would be the 1990s before Johnny Lightning produced the Bel Air and Alpine in 1:64. Corgi also released the Alpine. In 2002 Corgi finally produced a 1:43 scale Alpine as part of the Ultimate Bond Collection. The JBCC includes seven vehicles from the film: the Sunbeam; Bel Air; the Dragon 'tank' that guards Dr No's base (actually an armoured car as it has wheels not tracks); Ford Anglia; LaSalle hearse; Ford Consul; and an Austin A55 Cambridge Mark II taxi.

Dr No begins with Strangways being killed by a team of hitmen known as the Three Blind Mice as he is about to get into his Ford Anglia. In this case the film title printed on the base is incorrect. This is from JBCC.

The Three Blind Mice use a chauffeur-driven LaSalle hearse as a getaway car. Later they try to run Bond's Sunbeam off the road, but crash. This is from JBCC.

The first car Bond drives on screen is this 1957 Chevrolet Bel Air convertible, after getting the better of his driver, Mr Jones. This is from JBCC.

The JBCC Bel Air features a well-detailed interior. The glovebox is open, showing the pistol Mr Jones was reaching for, and Bond's bag is on the back seat.

Bond is taken to Strangways' house to look for clues by the Police Commissioner in his official Ford Consul Mark II. This is from JBCC.

Bond, on his way to meet villainess Miss Taro in his Sunbeam Alpine, is almost run off the road by the LaSalle hearse. This was the first real 'Bond Car', although it had no gadgets. The JBCC diorama is very detailed, with the pursuing LaSalle shown on the printed background.

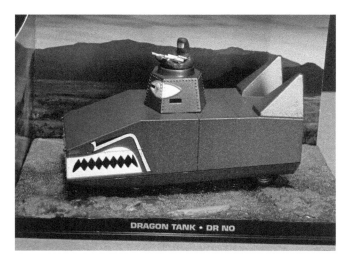

Crab Key, the island base of the sinister Dr No, is guarded by a fire-breathing dragon, which is actually an armoured car with a flamethrower in the nose. This is from JBCC.

From Russia With Love (1963), Sean Connery

A beautiful Russian defector with a decoding machine will only deal with Bond, but it is all a plot by Spectre. There is really no 'Bond Car' in this film. The 1930s Bentley 4¼ Litre (with car telephone) Bond takes on a picnic remains parked throughout its brief appearance; the only vehicle he drives, other than a motorboat, is a truck! Again, there were no contemporary models for the film. JL did the Ford station wagon in 1:64, and Corgi would eventually produce a model of the Chevrolet truck, nearly forty years after the film was released. The JBCC offers the best selection of models: the Bentley; a Citroen Traction Avant used to tail Bond; a Plymouth Savoy taxi; the Ford station wagon in its four-door form, and the Chevrolet Apache 1-ton truck. The back of this should really be filled with flowers (and a miniature version of Tatiana Romanova), but alas it is empty.

In *From Russia With Love* Bond has a Bentley, with a telephone, although he is not seen actually driving it. This is from JBCC.

Citroen Traction Avant, used by the Bulgarians to tail Bond in Istanbul, before being hijacked by assassin Red Grant, who is working for Spectre. This is from JBCC.

Ford Ranch Wagon; when first seen, on its way to the Gypsy camp, this is a four-door model, but in a later scene it has only two doors. Both the JBCC and JL produced the four-door version.

Chevrolet Apache 1-ton truck; this is the only vehicle Bond actually drives in the film, apart from a motorboat. This is from JBCC, also modelled by Corgi.

The grille of the JBCC Apache is highly detailed, with Chevrolet lettering and red 'bow-tie' badge, as well as lights and indicators.

Goldfinger (1964), Sean Connery

Auric Goldfinger 'loves only gold', and plans an attack on the US Bullion Depository at Fort Knox. This was the first film in which vehicles would play a major role, and the first with a proper 'Bond Car' – the DB5. Corgi have produced the DB5 in several sizes, Goldfinger's Rolls-Royce in two sizes, and reissued the small JL Mustang convertible driven by Tilly Masterson. JL did the DB5 and Mustang. Hot Wheels did Mainline and Entertainment versions of the DB5, while their Bond series included a '64 Lincoln Continental. The JBCC included a massive eleven models from this film, including two versions of the DB5, one with tyre slashers deployed for its battle with the Mustang, and one after the ejector seat has been fired. The remaining nine were: Ford Mustang convertible with the top down; Ford Thunderbird; Lincoln Continental; Ford Falcon Ranchero pickup; Rolls-Royce Phantom III Sedanca de Ville; Ford Country Squire station wagon; the Mercedes 220S used to chase the DB5 in Switzerland; Dodge M43 ambulance; and a Lincoln Continental convertible.

Auric Goldfinger's Rolls-Royce Phantom III Sedanca de Ville; parts of the car were made of gold, allowing him to use it for smuggling. This is the small Corgi model from their Showcase collection, which has 007 number plates.

The Rolls-Royce has an open driving compartment, and an enclosed passenger saloon. The JBCC model features Oddjob at the wheel, complete with bowler hat.

After Bond is captured in Switzerland, he is flown to Kentucky, and taken out to the Goldfinger estate in a Ford Country Squire station wagon. This is from JBCC.

CIA agent Felix Leiter provides backup for Bond while he is operating in America, using a Ford Thunderbird convertible. This is from JBCC.

Lincoln Continental, in which Oddjob drives gangster Mr Solo to the airport, but actually kills him, and puts the vehicle into a car crusher – the boot filled with gold. This is from JBCC.

After the Continental is crushed, the remains are loaded into the back of a Ford Falcon Ranchero pickup, and are driven back to the Goldfinger Stud Farm by Oddjob. This is from JBCC.

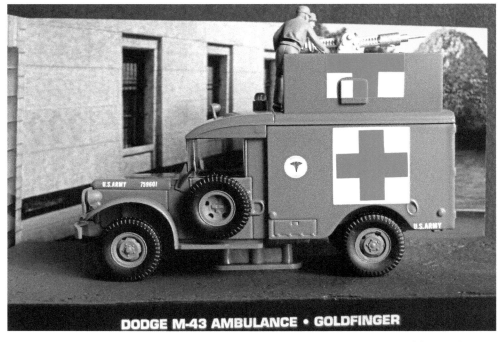

During the attack on Fort Knox, a convoy of fake Army vehicles drive up to the base. This Dodge M43 ambulance conceals a laser, which Goldfinger uses to cut his way into the Fort. This is from JBCC.

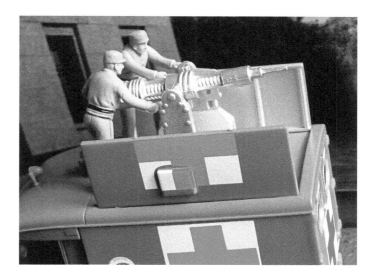

The roof of the ambulance opens, and the laser is raised into its firing position. The crew are shown preparing the laser for action. This is from JBCC.

Thunderball (1965), Sean Connery

A Royal Air Force Avro Vulcan bomber is hijacked by Spectre, along with its two nuclear bombs. Underwater action dominates this film, but there are still plenty of cars, and the DB5 makes its second appearance. There were no contemporary models for this film, apart from the Corgi DB5, which was really a *Goldfinger* model. Much later Corgi would produce *Thunderball* versions of the DB5, including a 50th Anniversary model. JL put their small DB5 on a *Thunderball* card (as did Corgi), and also released the Ford Mustang convertible. The JBCC includes seven models: a DB5 with water jets; the Ford Mustang convertible with top up; Ford Fairlane 500 Skyliner; Mercedes-Benz 190 Binz ambulance; another Ford Thunderbird; a Lincoln Continental stretched limousine; and a Morris Minor convertible. The Avro Vulcan plays a major role in the film, but although Corgi make Vulcans in different sizes, they have not done a Bond version. This means using a regular Vulcan model to represent the film aircraft.

In *Thunderball*, at the funeral of Spectre agent Jacques Boitier, his 'widow' (actually Boitier himself in disguise) is seen getting into a Lincoln Continental stretched limousine – but Bond is not fooled. This is from JBCC.

Emilio Largo attends a Spectre meeting in Paris in a Ford Thunderbird, which is now playing a villain car. This is from JBCC.

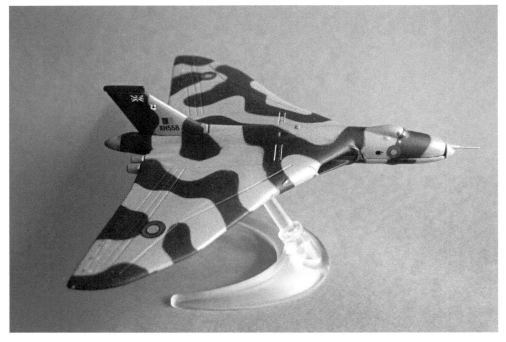

The RAF Avro Vulcan bomber plays a major role in the film, but there are no official Bond models. This is the small Corgi Vulcan B.2 on its display stand, although the markings are from a later period.

At the Shrublands Health Clinic, Bond sees a Mercedes-Benz 190 Binz ambulance delivering a body in the dead of night. This is from JBCC.

In the Bahamas, after checking out Largo's boat, Bond is given a lift to his hotel by villainess Fiona Volpe in her Ford Mustang convertible. This is from JBCC.

MORRIS MINOR CONVERTIBLE • THUNDERBALL

After a further reconnaissance mission, Bond is given another lift back to his hotel, but in a slightly less glamorous Morris Minor Tourer (convertible). This is from JBCC.

You Only Live Twice (1967), Sean Connery

After his death is faked, and he is 'buried' at sea, Bond is sent to Japan to foil another Spectre plot. There are few vehicles in this film, although Toyota provided a special convertible version of their 2000GT coupe. Corgi released their second Bond model in 1967, the Toyota. Since the film car did not have any gadgets beyond a video communications system, Corgi added a rocket battery in the boot. A catch on the left side opened the boot lid, while the rockets were fired by pressing down on either the left or right side, which launched the two rockets on that side. Pressing straight down fired a full salvo. There was also an accessory pack containing sixteen spare missiles. This model was later modified, and turned into a normal road car, without the missiles. Airfix released a kit of the Toyota in 1:24 scale. They also did the autogyro named *Little Nellie*, which Bond uses to search for the Spectre lair. It would take Corgi more than three decades to produce their own version of *Little Nellie*, but they then modelled her in two sizes. JL and Corgi both produced the Toyota in 1:64. Hot Wheels did a 2000GT coupe in their Mainline toy range; the Bond convertible version only being available in the Entertainment series. The JBCC only included three models from this film: the 2000GT, and the Toyota Crown villain car that gets dropped into the sea by a helicopter. *Little Nellie* was one of the three subscriber-only models, and did not come with the usual diorama. The vessel used for Bond's burial at sea is HMS *Tenby*, a Whitby class frigate. Tri-ang Minic Ships did a model of this vessel, and three of her sisters, in 1:1200.

The Toyota 2000GT in *You Only Live Twice* had no weapons, but Corgi gave it a rocket battery in the boot for increased play value. The catch on the left side opens the boot and pressing down on the model fires the rockets. This is a later reissue.

Hot Wheels had a Toyota 2000GT coupe in their standard toy range, but the Bond convertible was only available in the Entertainment series, these models having metal baseplates and more realistic wheels.

Toyota Crown villain car, chasing Bond and Aki in the 2000GT. It is about to be picked up by the KV-107 twin-rotor helicopter shown on the printed background and dropped into the sea. This is from JBCC.

The real star of the film is the heavily armed Wallis autogyro *Little Nellie*, which downs four Spectre helicopters in a dogfight. This is the small Showcase model from Corgi, although the figure is incorrectly dressed and should be wearing a white helmet.

Casino Royale (1967), David Niven

Someone is killing secret agents and Sir James Bond is brought out of retirement to find out who. This was the first of only two Bond films not made by Eon Productions. There are numerous vehicles, but most appear only fleetingly. Bond does have a Bentley, but there seems to be some doubt as to exactly what sort it is. There were no official models to tie in with this film, and it was not covered by the JBCC. At one point Bond in his Bentley is chased by a Jaguar E-Type convertible, and a milk float (a Bedford CA van with cut-out sides). There is also a Volkswagen pickup, based on the VW van. Bond's daughter uses a standard FX4 London taxi. Ordinary models of these could be used to represent the film vehicles.

On Her Majesty's Secret Service (1969), George Lazenby

Bond meets, and eventually marries, Tracy Di Vicenzo, but she is killed on their wedding day. Bond gets the latest Aston Martin, the DBS. At one point Bond and Tracy are being chased in her Mercury Cougar, and become involved in a stock car race. Pay attention during this sequence: some of the billboards around the track are for Corgi Models, and the two Minis in the race (one red, one green) have Corgi advertising on the edges of the roof. Corgi went all out for this film. Although there were no large-scale models, there were three Juniors and four Rockets, mainly depicting vehicles from the racing scene.

Above left: *On Her Majesty's Secret Service* saw Corgi release two versions of the Juniors bobsleigh, in different colours, for James Bond and Spectre. The picture in the centre of the card could be cut out and kept. (Vectis Auctions)

Above right: The Corgi Juniors Gift Set contained both versions of the bobsleigh, and a Volkswagen Beetle from the stock car race. All were on their normal cards, and were contained in an outer box. This is now one of the rarest Bond sets. (Vectis Auctions)

Right: The Corgi Rockets set contained four models: Tracy's Cougar, a Spectre Mercedes, a Ford Escort and a Ford Capri from the stock car race. Again, individually carded models were contained within an outer box. The key allowed the chassis to be removed. Boxed sets such as this are now very rare. (Vectis Auctions)

All came on cards, the Rockets having a key to remove the chassis. Two of the Juniors are bobsleighs – one for Bond, and one for Blofeld – which use the same casting. Strangely, there was no DBS for Bond, even though there was a DBS in the Rockets range. There were two boxed sets, each comprising the normal carded models in an outer box. These sets are now among the rarest and most expensive of all Bond diecasts. They did not have a long production life, and have never been reissued. There have been several models of Tracy's Cougar over the years, in various scales, including one by JL with the top down as it first appears, also released by Corgi, but most come with the top up. Corgi finally produced Bond's DBS in 1:36 in 2002 as part of The Ultimate Collection. The JBCC includes six models: the DBS; Cougar; Mercedes 220S; Mercedes 600; Volkswagen Beetle; and an Austin Mini from the race, adorned with Corgi logos.

Bond now drives an Aston Martin DBS, but it is only seen at the beginning and end of the film, and has no gadgets. This is the car in which Tracy is killed. This is from JBCC.

Tracy's Mercury Cougar convertible, with the top up and ski rack fitted, at the stock car race, showing considerable damage to the body. The Husky posters in the background are not visible in the film. This is from JBCC.

The Volkswagen Beetle in the JBCC was a different vehicle to the one modelled by Corgi, and was not from the stock car race, instead being used by MI6 agent Campbell.

Spectre agents use a sinister black Mercedes-Benz 220S when chasing Tracy's Cougar, but crash during the stock car race. This is from JBCC.

The JBCC only includes one vehicle from the race, a red Mini. On the roof are sponsor's logos for Corgi, and Corgi billboards are visible on the printed backscene, both of which are totally correct.

After Bond and Tracy are married, Blofeld and Irma Bunt arrive in a Mercedes 600 and kill Tracy. Blofeld is at the wheel, and wearing a neckbrace – a result of his bobsleigh battle with Bond. This is from JBCC.

Diamonds Are Forever (1971), Sean Connery

Bond is after stolen diamonds. Corgi were back with large-scale models, releasing the Moon Buggy that Bond 'borrows'. This had articulated arms, claws that really gripped, a radar scanner that rotated as the model moved, and a Bond figure that popped up when the cockpit cover was opened. Unfortunately, the model was rather delicate. They also did the Ford Mustang Mach 1 from the Las Vegas chase scene. This is the most commonly modelled vehicle from the film, with the JL example also being issued by Corgi. JL also did the Cadillac hearse, although it lacked the landau irons seen on the film car. Hot Wheels did the Mustang in both their Bond and Entertainment lines. The JBCC includes the Mustang and Moon Buggy, adding the Triumph Stag convertible Bond drives briefly, the Cadillac hearse and the Ford Econoline van. When Bond is using the Stag, he takes it across the English Channel on a hovercraft car ferry, *The Princess Margaret*. Airfix produced a 1:144 scale kit of this craft, the SRN4, to the same scale as their model airliners, with a clear roof to show off the interior, which would make an unusual 'Bond' model. The ocean liner SS *Canberra* appears at the end of the film. There was a 1:1200 diecast in the Minic Ships range, and a 1:600 plastic kit by Airfix.

Diamonds Are Forever sees Bond impersonating diamond smuggler Peter Franks, driving his Triumph Stag, and taking it to Amsterdam, where he meets Tiffany Case. This is from JBCC.

The Cadillac hearse, with landau irons, of Slumber Inc. The casket in the back contains the body of the real Peter Franks, and a stash of diamonds. This is from JBCC.

The Ford Econoline van; Bond stows away in the back in order to get inside a Whyte Tectronics plant, where he discovers the diamonds are being used in a space weapon. This is from JBCC.

The JBCC version of the Mustang on a diorama base, with rubbish bin and litter-strewn street. This is the most commonly modelled vehicle from the film.

The original Corgi version of the Ford Mustang Mach 1. Planned as a regular model, this just had opening doors, but no figures. Even the box had only a simple panel in one corner proclaiming its Bond connection. (Vectis Auctions)

Getting out of the Whyte Tectronics facility proves a little harder than getting in, and Bond has to steal a prototype Moon Buggy, which is under test. This is a reissued Corgi model; the original came in different colours, making it easy to tell the versions apart.

Live and Let Die (1973), Roger Moore

Bond is after a drug ring run by the Prime Minister of San Monique, a Caribbean island. The early 1970s were a quiet time for Corgi, and there were no contemporary models for the film, but things picked up in later years. JL did a Dodge Monaco, depicting the car of Sheriff J. W. Pepper. At one point Bond steals an old double-decker bus (no, it is not a Routemaster) belonging to San Monique Transport, and shears the top off going under a low bridge: Corgi eventually included a Leyland RT model in their Definitive Bond Collection. There were eight models in the JBCC: Corvorado; Mini Moke (which has appeared in several Bond films, usually painted yellow and lurking in the background as a villain car, but here given its moment in the sun); Chevrolet Nova police car; Chevrolet Impala convertible; Checker Marathon taxi; Chevrolet Impala Custom Coupe; Chevrolet Bel Air; and a police Bel Air. The Louisiana State Police cars in the film carry a variety of colour schemes, and have various types of flashing lights on the roof.

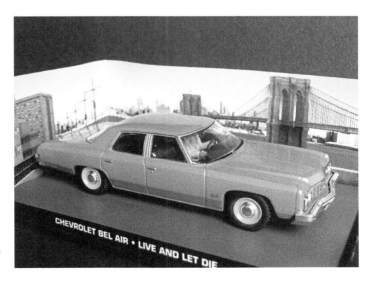

In *Live and Let Die* Bond is being driven into New York from the airport in this Chevrolet Bel Air when his driver is killed and he has to drive from the back seat. This is from JBCC.

The Corvorado was based on a Chevrolet Corvette, with a body resembling the Cadillac Eldorado. The red dot on the right door mirror is the dart gun used to kill the driver of Bond's Bel Air. This is from JBCC.

A Checker Marathon, the classic New York cab, used by Bond to trail drug dealer Mr Big. This is from JBCC.

The Mini Moke appeared in several Bond films, usually painted yellow and lurking in the background as a villain car, but here it finally gets its moment in the sun. This is from JBCC.

CHEVROLET IMPALA • LIVE AND LET DIE

On the Caribbean island of San Monique, Bond continues his investigations using a Chevrolet Impala convertible. This is from JBCC.

A San Monique Chevrolet Nova police car in hot pursuit of Bond and Solitaire in a stolen San Monique Transport double-decker bus. This is from JBCC – only Corgi have modelled the bus.

CHEVROLET BEL AIR POLICE CAR • LIVE AND LET DIE

Having just lost his own car in a collision with a boat, Sheriff Pepper commandeers this Louisiana State Police Bel Air. These cars display a variety of colour schemes, and different types of roof lights. This is from JBCC.

The Man With the Golden Gun (1974), Roger Moore

A hitman is apparently after Bond, and Bond is after him. Again, there were no contemporary models for the film. A model that is often described as an unofficial film tie-in is the Corgi Super Juniors E2009 Aerocar. There was a real flying car called the AVE Mizar, which combined a Ford Pinto car with the wings, tail unit and the rear piston engine of a Cessna Super Skymaster. The car could be detached from the aircraft portion for use on the ground, but the prototype crashed in 1973. The Corgi model is very similar to the Mizar, with the car also being detachable. Despite this it is absolutely, categorically, not the flying AMC Matador used by Scaramanga in the film. The shape is completely different, the film car has wingtip fuel tanks, and it is a jet, while the Mizar had a propeller. Some photos do show the Bond car with a propeller at the front, but only on the ground. In the film, and in flight, it is clearly a jet. JL did Bond's AMC Hornet, and an MGB convertible. Corgi eventually did the Hornet in 1:36. There were only four models in the JBCC: the MGB; Hornet; Scaramanga's Matador in its road form; and a white Mercedes-Benz 220.

The Corgi Super Juniors Aerocar bears only a slight resemblance to the flying car used by villain Scaramanga in *The Man With The Golden Gun*. Like the real AVE Mizar, the car can be detached from the wings. (Vectis Auctions)

In Hong Kong, Mary Goodnight picks up Bond from the ferry in her MGB. The JBCC models combine moulded plastic bases with printed backgrounds, giving even these small dioramas great depth.

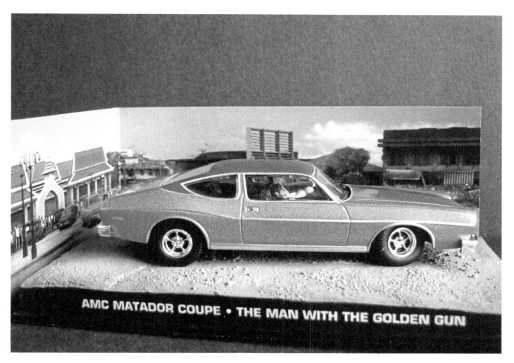

Scaramanga drives an AMC Matador that can be fitted with wings, allowing him to make a quick escape from Bond, with Mary Goodnight in the boot. The JBCC only depicted the vehicle in its normal road form.

Bond steals an AMC Hornet from a car showroom in Bangkok, Thailand, to chase Scaramanga and make a 360-degree roll while jumping a river. The Hornet has been modelled several times. This is from JBCC.

The Spy Who Loved Me (1977), Roger Moore

Bond and the beautiful Russian agent Triple X must join forces to find missing British and Soviet nuclear submarines. Corgi were back, with a host of models. Until now, they had only produced models in one size for each film – either full-sized Corgis, or Juniors – but from now on models would come in both sizes for each film. There was the Lotus Esprit in its submarine form, which actually ran on concealed wheels in the base, and the Stromberg Jetranger helicopter, the large model having a rocket battery under the fuselage, although the helicopter in the film was actually armed with machine guns. The models were available singly, or in large and small twin-packs. The Lotus models were also available in a Little and Large set. The small Lotus would later be made as a road car. Finally there was a Juniors Gift Set containing several models not available on their own. This contained the standard Lotus and Jetranger; a Mercedes (it should be a Ford), with paint over the windscreen as in the movie; a motor boat on a trailer; and the telephone repair van used by the villain Jaws. The Jaws van also turned up in a mixed Bond set, with models from several different movies. JL eventually produced the Lotus in its road form, reissued by Corgi, and the telephone van, which Corgi did not reissue. As already mentioned, the Corgi and JL vans were based on standard Chevrolet and Ford vans, not the Sherpa used in the film. The Corgi Showcase Lotus was again the submarine version. Hot Wheels included the Esprit in the Mainline, Bond, and Entertainment ranges, but the submarine version was only available in the Entertainment series. The JBCC saw five models, including road and submarine versions of the Lotus; the telephone van, this time correctly modelled as a Leyland Sherpa; Ford Taunus from the road chase; and the Kawasaki Z900 motorcycle with explosive sidecar. The end of the film sees Bond and Triple X being picked up by the Royal Navy assault ship HMS *Fearless*, available in 1:600 from Airfix.

In *The Spy Who Loved Me*, the steel-toothed killer Jaws poses as a telephone repairman. The JBCC model correctly shows his van as a Leyland Sherpa, while the smaller Corgi Junior was based on their standard Chevrolet Van casting and Johnny Lightning used a Ford.

Bond and Soviet agent Triple X use this Lotus Esprit in Sardinia, and are attacked in turn by a motorcycle, a Ford Taunus and a Jetranger helicopter. This is from JBCC.

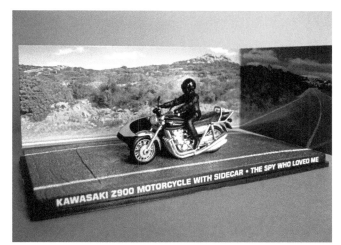

The Kawasaki Z900 motorcycle combination; the sidecar is actually a detachable, rocket-powered bomb, which is launched against the Esprit. This is from JBCC.

The Bell Jetranger helicopter flown by Naomi in the attack on the Lotus Esprit. The real helicopter was armed with twin machine guns under the fuselage, but the Corgi model has rockets. This is a reissue of the large Corgi model; there was also a Juniors version.

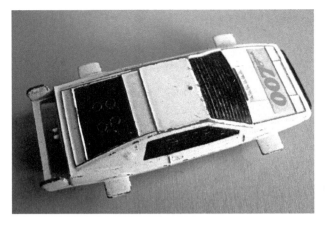

Escaping from the Jetranger, the Esprit drives off a pier into the sea: and converts into a submarine. Again, Corgi produced both regular and Junior-sized versions, which were also available in a Little and Large set. This slightly playworn example is a Junior.

Moonraker (1979), Roger Moore

Bond makes it into space aboard the Moonraker rocket, which is actually the Space Shuttle then being developed for NASA. Corgi released their Shuttle in both large and small versions. The Jetranger helicopter also reappeared in two sizes, in the colours of Drax Airlines. The Showcase collection later included another Shuttle. Corgi Shuttles were only available as the basic Orbiter. The Full Stack version, with External Tank and two Solid Rocket Boosters, ready for launch, were made by Dinky and ERTL, but only in NASA colours. ERTL also did the Shuttle Carrier Aircraft – a modified Boeing 747 airliner with the Shuttle carried atop the fuselage – which is seen at the beginning of the film. Both Airfix in Britain and Revell in America produced 1:144 scale kits of the Moonraker Shuttle in Full Stack form, with Revell also doing the Orbiter on its own. The only JL model for the film was the 1930s Hispano-Suiza. The JBCC included five models: the MP Lafer; Hispano-Suiza; Rolls-Royce Silver Shadow I; Chevrolet C10 ambulance; and the Bondola, a Venetian gondola that converts into a hovercraft.

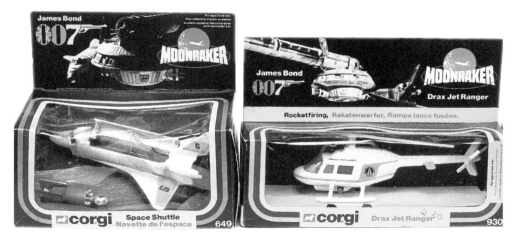

For *Moonraker* Corgi produced both the Moonraker space shuttle and another version of their Jetranger helicopter. These models were available individually, or in a set. There were also Juniors versions of both models, and a Juniors twin-pack. (Vectis Auctions)

The later Corgi Showcase version of the Moonraker Shuttle lacked the opening cargo bay doors of the two previous models, but did have a retractable undercarriage.

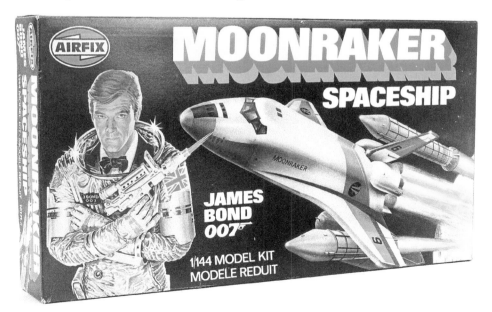

Both Airfix in Britain, and Revell in America, produced plastic kits of the Moonraker Shuttle. These showed the craft ready for launch, with the central External Tank, and two Solid Rocket Boosters. Revell also released the Orbiter on its own. (Vectis Auctions)

Bond is given a lift to the airport in this 1930s Hispano-Suiza belonging to villain Hugo Drax. This is from JBCC, but it was also modelled by JL.

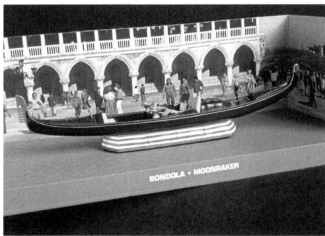

In Venice, Bond travels by gondola, which is clearly a Q Branch special, being much faster than a normal gondola and capable of converting into a hovercraft. The JBCC model is smaller than the usual 1:43.

Arriving in Rio aboard an Air France Concorde, Bond travels briefly in a Rolls-Royce Silver Shadow I, and is followed by a Lafer. This is from JBCC.

The MP Lafer was a Brazilian-built sports car resembling a British MG, but using Volkswagen parts. In Rio, Manuela follows Bond in his Rolls-Royce. This is from JBCC.

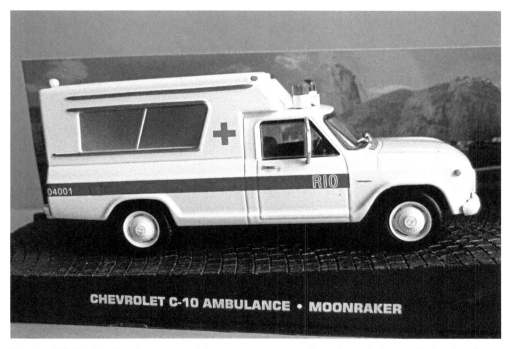

Bond and Holly Goodhead are captured, but manage to escape from this ambulance, which is based on a Chevrolet C10 pickup truck. This is from JBCC.

For Your Eyes Only (1981), Roger Moore

A British spy ship is sunk, and Bond must recover its communications equipment. One of the less glamorous Bond cars was the Citroen 2CV. Corgi released this in both large and small versions, and in a Little and Large set. The Lotus Esprit returns, in its Turbo version. There are actually two cars – the white one that gets blown up early on, and a bronze one with ski racks. This was the only film for which JL produced three models, although two were simply the Lotus in different colours, with Corgi reissuing the bronze one. The third model was the Topper Sand Stormer, representing the two beach buggies that attack Bond and Countess Lisl, although it is a very poor match. Corgi eventually produced the Lotus Esprit Turbo in 1:36. The JBCC provides seven models: a very battered 2CV; both versions of the Lotus; a much better GP Beach Buggy; the Peugeot 504; Mercedes-Benz 200D and 450 SEL. Citroen were so pleased to have their 2CV featured in the film that they released a Limited Edition of the real car, complete with 007 logos and fake bullet holes. While it is not strictly a film car, there have been several models of this version, and it is a very attractive model.

The star of *For Your Eyes Only* was the little Citroen 2CV. Corgi produced both regular and Junior versions, which came in a variety of packaging styles. There was also a Little and Large twin-pack. (Vectis Auctions)

The Mercedes-Benz 450 SEL might look rather strange, apparently wedged in a stone wall, but it has actually just crashed and is hanging precariously over a cliff edge. This is from JBCC.

Chasing the 2CV through the olive groves were a pair of Peugeot 504 villain cars, one of which ends up in a tree. This is from JBCC.

Bond has two Lotus Esprit Turbos in this film, but neither does anything very exciting. As a model, this bronze version is far more common than the white one seen earlier. This is from JBCC.

The villains have a Mercedes-Benz 200D. The JBCC model includes snow chains on the rear wheels, although these are only printed on, not moulded.

Bond and Countess Lisl (played by Cassandra Harris, wife of future Bond Pierce Brosnan) are attacked on the beach by a pair of GP Beach Buggies, and the Countess is killed. This is the JBCC version, which is far more accurate than the one by JL.

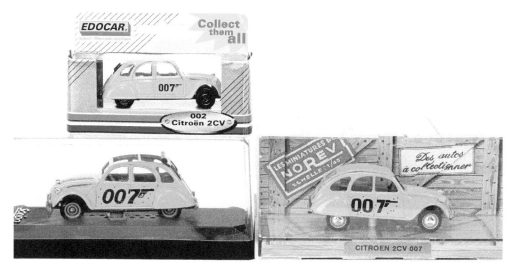

Not actually a movie car; Citroen produced a special Limited Edition of the real 2CV, with Bond logos and fake bullet holes. This has been modelled by several different companies: here are examples by Edocar, Solido, and Norev. (Vectis Auctions)

Octopussy (1983), Roger Moore

A Soviet general uses the Octopussy circus to smuggle an atomic bomb onto a US air base in West Germany. The opening scene sees Bond flying a tiny BD5 jet, which had been hidden inside a horsebox, towed by a Range Rover convertible. Corgi released the combination as a Juniors-sized Gift Set. Unfortunately there was no large-scale

The Junior-sized Corgi *Octopussy* set contained the Range Rover convertible, horsebox and Bede BD5 Acrostar jet from the opening sequence. (Vectis Auctions)

The JBCC version of the Range Rover, with Bianca at the wheel, just after Bond has unhitched the horsebox containing the BD5.

version. The Japanese firm of LS also did a 1:72 kit of the BD5. At one point, Bond is chasing the Octopussy circus train in a Mercedes that has lost its tyres, allowing it to take to the rails. Corgi eventually modelled this car, and the first version included a length of railway track, which was deleted from later issues. When Bond is trying to get to the USAF base, he is given a lift by a German couple in a Volkswagen, which was modelled by JL. The JBCC included nine models: Mercedes 250SE on rails; Tuk Tuk taxi; Willys Jeep M606; BMW 518 police car; Alfa Romeo GTV6; the BD5 Acrostar mini-jet; Range Rover convertible; Austin FX4 taxi; and a Volga M24.

The BD5 jet soon runs out of fuel, so Bond lands at the nearest petrol station for a top-up. The JBCC model is shown with both the wings and tailplanes folded.

In India the three-wheel Tuk Tuk is used as a taxi, but this is an MI6 'company car' with increased performance. This is from JBCC.

Bond is able to escape from the clutches of Kamal Khan by posing as a dead body, which is loaded aboard this Willys Jeep for disposal. This is from JBCC.

The Octopussy Circus is being used to smuggle an atomic bomb onto a USAF air base. Bond chases their train in a Mercedes-Benz 250SE he 'borrows' from General Orlov. Both the JBCC and the early Corgi models showed the car running on railway tracks.

As Bond races to avert disaster, his stolen Alfa Romeo GTV6 is chased by West German police cars and motorcycles, including the BMW 518. This is from JBCC.

Never Say Never Again (1983), Sean Connery

This was the second of the non-Eon films. It was a low-budget remake of *Thunderball*, with very few vehicles. This time a pair of Air Launched Cruise Missiles are hijacked after launch from a US B-1 bomber. Bond is seen briefly in a Bentley, then gets a Yamaha XJ650 motorcycle, while the chief villainess has a Renault 5 Turbo. There have been no official Bond models for this film, and it was not included in the JBCC, so non-Bond versions of suitable vehicles will again have to fill the gaps.

A View To A Kill (1985), Roger Moore

Bond must stop a plot to corner the world computer chip market by destroying Silicon Valley with an earthquake. There were no Corgi models for this film, as Matchbox

For *A View To A Kill* Matchbox had the Bond licence, and they produced two models for the film: a Renault 11 taxi, and a Rolls-Royce Silver Cloud II, both in small window boxes. (Vectis Auctions)

Bond gives chase to assassin May Day after she has parachuted from the Eiffel Tower, in a Renault 11 taxi, which is soon reduced to a wreck. This is from JBCC.

now held the licence. There were two models in the usual Matchbox size, but in special boxes: the Renault 11 taxi Bond uses to chase villainess May Day after she parachutes from the Eiffel Tower; and the Rolls-Royce Silver Cloud II he uses when undercover. Both of these models would later be included in the regular Matchbox line. An Action Pack, or Gift Set, with four models was planned but not issued. Prototypes of this do exist, and some collectors have made up their own sets containing regular Matchbox models. When Corgi regained the Bond licence they issued the Renault taxi in 1:36. JL did the Corvette of Russian agent Pola Ivanova, as did HW as part of the Entertainment series. There were six models in the JBCC: Chevrolet Corvette; Renault 11 taxi; US Dodge Monaco police car; Renault Fuego Turbo; and Rolls-Royce Silver Cloud II. Gift 2 was the taxi after it has lost its top, and been cut in half.

Bond's chase of May Day proves catastrophic for the Renault, which first losses its roof, and is then cut in half. This was the second of three subscriber-only models in the JBCC, and the only one to come with a diorama.

Going undercover, Bond uses a chauffeur-driven Rolls-Royce Silver Cloud II. This was actually the personal car of Bond producer Cubby Broccoli, although not the one that ends up in a lake. This is from JBCC.

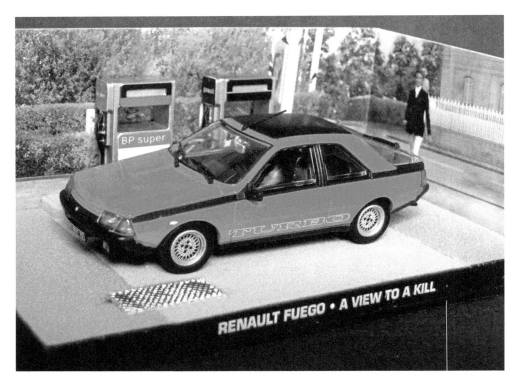

Bond's chauffeur is killed when he takes the Rolls-Royce to a car wash, having been followed by this Renault Fuego Turbo. This is from JBCC.

Both Bond and the Russians are interested in villain Max Zorin, this Chevrolet Corvette belonging to Russian agent Pola Ivanova. This is from JBCC.

Having stolen a San Francisco Fire Department American LaFrance ladder truck, Bond is pursued by numerous police cars, including this Dodge Monaco. This is from JBCC.

The Living Daylights (1987), Timothy Dalton

A defecting KGB general is not all he seems. Matchbox produced no models for this film at all. Much later Corgi released the Aston Martin V8 with extending skis in 1:36, and a smaller model in the ex-JL series. JL did the V8, as well as the yellow Red Crescent ambulance in which the drugged Bond is carried aboard a Hercules transport. This model is based on a normal Chevrolet van, and lacks the windows on the right side of the ambulance. It also has the words 'Protection Civile' on both sides, but the writing should be in Arabic on the right side. Even so, this is a very attractive model, especially if you only look at the left side. The JBCC contains eight models: Aston Martin V8 in both open Volante and enclosed Vantage forms; Lada 1500 police car; Land Rover Series III; Land Rover Lightweight; Audi 200 Quattro; VAZ-2105 unmarked police car; and one of my favourite Bond models, the Wales & Edwards Rangemaster milk float. Given the large part played in the film by the Lockheed C-130 Hercules, it deserves to be included too.

The Living Daylights opens on Gibraltar, with a hitman killing a double-O agent, then trying to escape in a stolen British Army Land Rover, with Bond clinging to the back. The scene is captured in the JBCC diorama.

Czechoslovakian Lada 1500 police cars appear in several scenes; this one has just had its body cut from the chassis by a laser on Bond's new Aston Martin. This is from JBCC.

A Russian KGB general apparently defects to the British, with Bond driving the Audi 200 Quattro getaway car. This is from JBCC.

To get past security at the MI6 safehouse, the deadly Necros poses as a milkman, using a Wales & Edwards Rangemaster electric milk float – one of the slowest vehicles ever to appear in a Bond movie. This is from JBCC.

Bond arrives at the MI6 safehouse in an Aston Martin V8 Volante (convertible) – there is even a hamper from Harrods on the back seat. This is from JBCC.

The Aston Martin is later fitted with a roof by Q Branch, turning it into a V8 Vantage. Other fittings include outrigger skis and various weapons. This is from JBCC.

Making their escape from a damaged Hercules transport plane in this Land Rover Lightweight, Bond and Kara head off to Karachi for dinner. This is from JBCC.

Licence To Kill (1989), Timothy Dalton

Bond goes rogue to hunt down a drug lord named Sanchez. This was the first Bond movie that children, at least in Britain, were not allowed to see. Its 15 Certificate meant no one under 15 could see it, which probably did not help toy sales. Later films were given a 12 Certificate. Elsewhere, the films remained open to children. Matchbox produced a four-piece Gift Set, the models adorned with 007 logos. One was a regular Matchbox miniature; one a heavy truck from the Convoy series; and two were aircraft from the Sky-Busters range. The plane in the set is a mix of three different light aircraft from the film: the red and white Cessna in which Sanchez tries to escape; the blue and white Cessna floatplane; and the Piper Cub crop-duster from the final truck chase, registration XB-LOX. The helicopter hardly resembles the US Coast Guard Aerospatiale HH-65A from the opening scenes. The pickup is the wrong type, and has flames on it, depicting the scene where it drives through blazing wreckage. The best model is the Kenworth tanker, although the sleeper cab is too tall. Corgi later produced a more accurate model of the Kenworth. JL did the white Jeep that gets crushed by one of the tankers. There were just three models in the JBCC: the Maserati Biturbo 425; Rolls-Royce Silver Shadow II; and the Dodge Ram pickup, although the body is length is wrong.

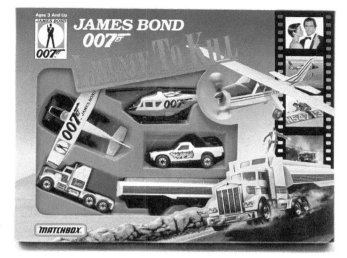

The Matchbox set for *Licence To Kill* contained four models, but only the Kenworth tanker actually resembled the vehicle it represented, while the Cessna combined the colours, registration letters and float undercarriage of three different aircraft. Neither the helicopter nor the pickup were close to accurate, but the box was really nice. (Vectis Auctions)

Bond uses a Rolls-Royce Silver Shadow II while undercover in Isthmus City, which is at one point driven by Q. This is from JBCC.

Maserati Biturbo 425 used by Sanchez, the man Bond is after. A shoulder-fired Stinger surface-to-air missile launcher is visible in the open boot. This is from JBCC.

A fleet of Kenworth tankers are being used by Sanchez to smuggle drugs. The Corgi model correctly has a normal-height sleeper cab, unlike the Matchbox version, which has a tall sleeper compartment. (Vectis Auctions)

The Dodge Ram pickup truck from the tanker chase, which drives through the blazing wreckage of one of the tankers. The vehicle in the film is a normal length version, while the JBCC model incorrectly has a long wheelbase.

GoldenEye (1995), Pierce Brosnan

GoldenEye is a space weapon, emitting an Electromagnetic Pulse, which destroys electronics. Goldeneye (with a small e) was the Jamaican holiday home of writer Ian Fleming, where he wrote all the Bond books. Bond was back after six years, and Corgi were back after twelve. There were two contemporary models for the film. Corgi put their standard 1:36 James Bond DB5 in a *GoldenEye* box and paired it with the Ferrari 355, which races the DB5 in the opening scene, but in 1:43, so the models did not match. Only later did they do the BMW Z3 in 1:36, and a smaller version in the Showcase range. JL did both the DB5 and Z3, with Corgi also releasing the DB5. The Franco-German Tiger helicopter plays a significant role in the film. Siku of Germany produce models in two sizes: 1:50, and a smaller, Matchbox-sized version. The JBCC includes six models: BMW Z3; Ferrari F355; ZAZ-965A; GAZ Volga; and VAZ-2106 police car. The Russian Army T-55 tank Bond drives through St Petersburg, in the best movie tank chase ever, was the third of the subscriber-only Gift models, and did not come with the usual diorama. It was made to 1:50 – a common scale for diecast military vehicles.

GoldenEye saw Bond driving an Aston Martin DB5 for the first time in thirty years. Corgi put their standard 1:36 DB5 in a special box for the film.

Villainess Xenia Onatopp pits her Ferrari 355 against the DB5. The superbly detailed JBCC model even features tiny Ferrari logos on the wheel hubs and the centre of the steering wheel.

The Eurocopter Tiger is actually an army attack helicopter, but in *GoldenEye* it is stolen from the flight deck of a French warship. This is the smaller of two Siku models, neither of which comes in Bond packaging.

The BMW Z3 has been modelled several times, despite not doing a great deal in the film. This is the small Corgi Showcase model; they also did a larger version in 1:36.

Jack Wade, Bond's CIA contact in St Petersburg, drives a small Russian ZAZ-965A, seen here with Bond's suitcase on the roofrack. This is from JBCC.

Escaping from General
Ourumov, Bond pursues the
general through St Petersburg
in a T-55 tank that just
happened to be parked nearby.
The JBCC subscriber-only
model is to 1:50 scale, and
comes without a diorama.

General Ourumov throws
Natalya into the back of his
GAZ Volga and attempts to
flee, with Bond giving chase
in a T-55, JBCC.

VAZ-2106 Russian police
cars and Army vehicles chase
Bond, but most are soon
destroyed. This is from JBCC.

Tomorrow Never Dies (1997), Pierce Brosnan

Bond battles a demented media magnate. Corgi reboxed their DB5, and later produced the BMW 750iL saloon in 1:36. JL also did the DB5 and what they described simply as 'Carver's Goons' Car' – a standard Chevrolet Impala SS model painted to match one of the cars destroyed by the 750iL during the battle in a parking building. There were only three models in the JBCC: the 750iL with weapons deployed and a large hole in the windscreen; Range Rover 4.6 HSE; and a Mercedes-Benz S-Class. BMW themselves released a Bond model of the big R1200C motorcycle that is chased by the Range Rovers through Saigon (which had been renamed Ho Chi Minh City way back in 1976), but there are other versions of this bike available.

In *Tomorrow Never Dies* Bond has a well-equipped BMW 750iL. The JBCC model shows him driving by remote control from the back seat, with all weapons deployed.

In a parking building a pair of Mercedes-Benz S-Class villain cars try to take on Bond and his BMW. This is from JBCC.

Bond and Chinese agent Wai Lin flee from Carver's men in Saigon on a BMW R1200C motorcycle. The company heavily promoted its involvement with the Bond films, issuing a number of Bond models in BMW-branded boxes. (Vectis Auctions)

Chasing the R1200C through the crowded streets are a pair of Range Rovers. Well-detailed figures add considerably to the feeling of action in these JBCC models.

The World Is Not Enough (1999), Pierce Brosnan

Bond is assigned to find who killed a major industrialist – it turns out to be his daughter Elektra. Corgi did the BMW Z8 in 1:36, and JL did a small-scale version in 1:64. There were five models from the JBCC, two of them being very exotic subjects; the expected Z8, modelled as it is being attacked by a helicopter with a multi-bladed logging saw; the Q Boat; Parahawk; Rolls-Royce Silver Shadow II; and Lada Niva. The Parahawk has a detachable, parachute-like wing, allowing it to fly, but on the ground it has skis for travelling over snow, which is how it was modelled.

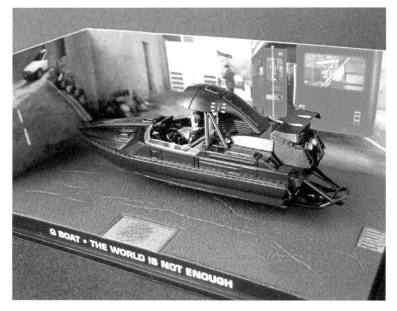

In *The World Is Not Enough*, Q builds this speedboat for his retirement, but Bond borrows it for a chase down the river Thames – and the surrounding streets. One of the more unusual models in the JBCC.

The main Bond car is a BMW Z8, with all the usual refinements. In the battle at the caviar factory Bond is able to shoot down one helicopter armed with a logging saw, but his Z8 is cut in half by a second. This is from JBCC.

The Parahawk is a ski-mobile with a detachable, parachute-like wing, four of which try to kill Bond in the mountains of Azerbaijan. This is from JBCC.

LADA NIVA • THE WORLD IS NOT ENOUGH

A mud-spattered Lada Niva driven by Davidoff, with Bond hiding in the back. This is from JBCC.

During the battle at the caviar factory between the Z8 and the helicopters, this unfortunate Rolls-Royce Silver Shadow II falls into the harbour. This is from JBCC.

Die Another Day (2002), Pierce Brosnan

Bond is captured on a mission in North Korea, and later exchanged. Corgi did the two cars from the big battle on the ice lake: the Aston Martin V12 Vanquish, and the Jaguar XKR. These were available in two sizes, regular and Showcase. JL only produced the Vanquish, but their second model from the film was one of their most unusual. The Bombardier Ski-Doo snowmobile is used by the ice palace guards in Iceland, and briefly by Bond. Seven vehicles were featured in the JBCC, but two are really only background vehicles, forming part of the exotic car collection of the villainous Colonel Moon: the Vanquish; Jaguar; Ford Thunderbird; Lamborghini Diablo; Ford Fairlane 500 Skyliner; Ford GT40; and another exotic model, the Osprey 5 hovercraft.

Seen only briefly at the beginning of *Die Another Day*, this Ford GT40 is part of Colonel Moon's exotic car collection. This is from JBCC.

A Lamborghini Diablo is also part of Colonel Moon's collection; it eventually ends up nose-down in the mud after falling out of an Antonov transport plane. This is from JBCC.

Colonel Moon is an arms dealer with various items for sale, including a fleet of Osprey 5 hovercraft. This is from JBCC.

During a brief visit to Cuba, Bond drives a 1950s Ford Fairlane 500 Skyliner convertible. This is from JBCC.

Bond again has a well-equipped Aston Martin, this time a V12 Vanquish, which does battle with a Jaguar on a frozen lake in Iceland. This is from JBCC.

Working for the US National Security Agency, Jinx drives a modern version of the Ford Thunderbird while on assignment in Iceland. This is from JBCC.

In the world of James Bond, driving a Jaguar means you are a villain, and this XKR has just as much weaponry as anything Bond himself might drive. This is from JBCC.

The small Showcase Jaguar XKR from Corgi, with its Gatling gun ready for action. The Showcase range also included a Vanquish.

Casino Royale (2006), Daniel Craig

The third version of this tale, but the first by Eon Productions – Bond takes on villain Le Chiffre at the gambling tables. Corgi produced a new 1:36 model of the left-hand drive DB5 that appears in the film, along with the new DBS. Both cars were included in various Gift Sets. There were also smaller models in the Showcase series. Hot Wheels had the DBS in their five-piece James Bond and Entertainment ranges. There were seven models in the JBCC: the DBS V12; Jaguar XJ8; Daimler Limousine; Range Rover Sport; Land Rover Defender; Ford Crown Victoria police car; and a ZIL-117 (seen only briefly, with a body in the boot).

Casino Royale opens with a trio of Land Rover Defenders carrying the villain Le Chiffre to a meeting in the jungles of Uganda. This is from JBCC.

RANGE ROVER SPORT • CASINO ROYALE

At the Ocean Club in the Bahamas, Bond drives this Range Rover Sport into a line of parked cars to set off their alarms, distracting the club security guards. This is from JBCC.

FORD CROWN VICTORIA POLICE INTERCEPTOR • CASINO ROYAL

In an attempt to blow up the prototype Skyfleet S570 airliner at Miami airport, a saboteur steals this Ford Crown Victoria police car, and then a fuel tanker, before being stopped by Bond. This is from JBCC.

DAIMLER LIMOUSINE • CASINO ROYALE

Bond and Vesper Lynd are picked up from the railway station and are taken to the Hotel Splendide in this Daimler limousine. This is from JBCC.

In the Hotel Splendide car park Bond finds his new Aston Martin DBS V12 waiting for him, although it lacks the usual Bond gadgets. This is from JBCC.

Being a Bond film, the villain Mr White naturally drives a Jaguar - in this case an XJ8 saloon. This is from JBCC.

Quantum of Solace (2008), Daniel Craig

A straight sequel to *Casino Royale*, with Bond battling another secret organisation – Quantum. Corgi simply reissued their existing DBS in a new box. This was the last film to be covered in depth by the JBCC, and they released nine models: starting with the intact DBS that appears at the very beginning; Ford Ka; Alfa Romeo 159 (two of which chase the DBS in the opening scene); Land Rover Defender of the Italian Carabinieri; Daimler Super Eight; Range Rover Sport; Ford Edge; Ford Bronco II; and finally a crash-damaged version of the DBS, with its left door ripped off and a good many dents.

Quantum of Solace opens with the DBS V12 being chased through a road tunnel and into a quarry, picking up a good deal of damage along the way. Both intact and damaged versions were included in the JBCC.

Chasing both Bond and his pursuers is a Land Rover Defender of the Italian Carabinieri, but it soon crashes. This is from JBCC.

The Ford Ka is driven by Camille, who picks up Bond thinking he is a geologist, and is chased through the streets of Port-au-Prince, Haiti. This is from JBCC.

Several models in the JBCC have been given a weathered finish to accurately depict how the vehicles looked on scene, including this very dusty Ford Bronco II pickup, briefly driven by Bond when trailing villain Dominic Greene.

In Bolivia, Bond drives this Range Rover Sport, failing to notice his friend Mathis has been dumped in the back – until pulled over by local police. This is from JBCC.

Skyfall (2012), Daniel Craig

A former MI6 agent is out for revenge, with a final battle at the Bond ancestral home in Scotland – Skyfall. The DB5 appears again, and has a bigger role than it has had in a long time, but is blown up by the villains. Contemporary models for each new Bond film are generally restricted to the main glamour cars. It usually takes a few years before other models begin appearing, hence the current lack of models for the last two movies. Corgi again reissued their DB5. The Hot Wheels Bond and Entertainment lines both included the existing DB5 on new cards. In 2012 the Italian company Italeri issued a Skyfall version of their 1:72 scale AgustaWestland AW101 kit – this being the helicopter used in the assault on Skyfall. Italeri have also branched out into diecast aircraft, releasing a 1:100 AW101 model. As the undercarriage is retracted, the model can only be displayed in flight on its display stand.

The only model in the JBCC for *Skyfall* was an existing model from the series – a rather plain version of the DB5 on a road in the Scottish Highlands.

Hot Wheels also put their existing Entertainment series DB5 on a new card, but it was painted a lighter shade of silver than the *Goldfinger* car.

The AgustaWestland AW101 helicopter is used by the villains in an attack on Skyfall manor in Scotland; this is the excellent Italeri diecast in 1:100 on its display stand. They also did a plastic kit in 1:72.

Spectre (2015), Daniel Craig

Blofeld is back. So far we have not had many models for this film, just the DB10, specially built for the film by Aston Martin, from Corgi and Hot Wheels. Corgi also produced a Spectre twin-pack, containing both the DB5 and DB10 in 1:36. Even the main villain car, the experimental Jaguar C-X75, is yet to appear. If you really want a C-X75, Scalextric did a 1:32 *Spectre* slot car set containing one, along with the DB10.

Corgi *Spectre* set in 1:36 containing the DB5 and DB10, both with opening doors, but no super-spy gadgets.

The Hot Wheels Mainline DB10; a simple toy, but still a first class model of the latest Bond car. There is also a more detailed version in the Entertainment series.

Card variations for the basic Hot Wheels DB10, with one showing a slightly cropped version of the main artwork. The actual models are identical.

James Bond Jr

No, not the son of James Bond, but his nephew. A teenager who attends the Warfield Academy, and battles the forces of SCUM (Saboteurs and Criminals United in Mayhem) – a junior version of Spectre. This carton series aired in 1991–92, and ran for sixty-five episodes. Many of the Bond film villains turned up on the show. ERTL released three diecasts based on the series: James' Car, an open sports car resembling a Ferrari; the insect-like SCUM Helicopter; and the Warfield Van, with pop-out wings.